LIGHTNING BOLT BOOKS™

Spooky Ghost Ships

T0386291

Walt Brody

Lerner Publications ◆ Minneapolis

Lerner Publications Company
An imprint of Lerner Publishing Group, Inc.
241 First Avenue North
Minneapolis, MN 55401 USA

For reading levels and more information, look up this title at www.lernerbooks.com.

Editor: Shee Yang

Library of Congress Cataloging-in-Publication Data

Names: Brody, Walt, 1978- author.
Title: Spooky ghost ships / Walt Brody.
Description: Minneapolis : Lerner Publications, 2021. | Series: Lightning bolt books—spooked! | Includes bibliographical references and index. | Audience: Ages 6-9 | Audience: Grades 2-3 | Summary: "You've heard the myths surrounding ghost ships, but are they really true? Simultaneously creepy, fascinating, and kid-friendly, this book explores the truth behind the myths—but beware: discover at your own risk!"— Provided by publisher.
Identifiers: LCCN 2019035035 (print) | LCCN 2019035036 (ebook) | ISBN 9781541596870 (library binding) | ISBN 9781728400525 (ebook)
Subjects: LCSH: Ghosts—Juvenile literature. | Ships—Miscellanea—Juvenile literature.
Classification: LCC BF1486 .B76 2021 (print) | LCC BF1486 (ebook) | DDC 133.1/22—dc23

LC record available at https://lccn.loc.gov/2019035035
LC ebook record available at https://lccn.loc.gov/2019035036

Manufactured in the United States of America
1-47793-48233-11/7/2019

Table of Contents

What Are Ghost Ships?

In October 2016, a ship appeared on Lake Superior. Then the ship suddenly vanished. This was a ghost ship.

Stories about ghost ships are based on real ships. Many ghost ships disappeared. Others were found with no crew. **All ghost ship stories are mysteries.**

Some ghost ships have no crew aboard.

Some ghost ships are thought to be haunted by the ghosts of crew members or passengers.

Stories about ghost ships go back hundreds of years. Some of these stories have become myths.

Ghost Ship Myths

The story of the *Flying Dutchman* is a myth. In 1641, the ship ran into a storm while sailing near Africa. The ship's captain tried to sail through the storm.

The ship was no match for the storm and sank. Since then, many people have claimed to see the *Flying Dutchman* ghost ship.

The *Flying Dutchman* was named after its Dutch captain.

The story of *Mary Celeste* is also a myth. The ship set sail in 1872. A week later, another ship following a similar route saw something large moving ahead. It was the *Mary Celeste.*

The *Mary Celeste*'s entire crew was missing. The ship's cargo was still there along with plenty of food and water. What happened to the crew is a mystery.

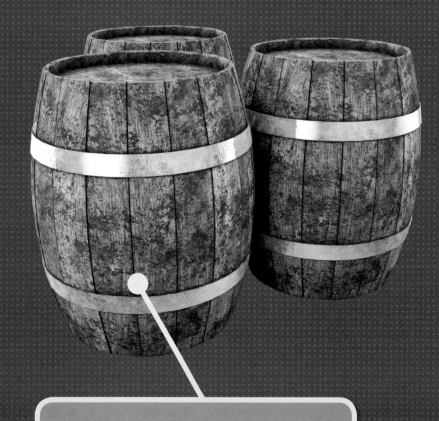

The *Mary Celeste* had valuable cargo on board.

Modern Ghost Ships

The *Sam Ratulangi PB 1600* is a cargo ship. In 2018, it was found at sea near Myanmar with no crew aboard.

Ship junkyards like this one can be full of abandoned ships.

The ship had been missing for nine years. It might have drifted away from a ship junkyard.

Another ghost ship story tells of a fishing boat near the northwestern coast of Australia in 2003. The *High Aim Number 6* was drifting with no crew aboard.

The *High Aim Number 6* was found drifting, just like this ship.

High Aim Number 6 carried 10 tons (9.1 t) of valuable tuna. What happened to the crew of this ghost ship?

Are Ghost Ships Real?

Most ghost ships are found with no crew or record of what happened to them. We may never know the truth about some ghost ships.

Many causes may explain why a ship lost its crew. A storm may have washed them away. Pirates may have come on board and taken the crew somewhere else.

Some people claim to see ghost ships disappear. But those ghost ships are most likely mirages.

A mirage is something that seems real but isn't.

Science has an answer for most ghost ship stories. So don't be scared if you see a ghostly ship in the distance!

Ghost Ship Encounter

Queen Mary was a luxury ship. It moved troops during World War II (1939–1945) and carried the rich and famous around the world. Sometimes people died on the *Queen Mary*. Some people believe the ship is haunted. It became a museum in 1967. You can find the truth for yourself. *Queen Mary* ghost tours have become popular with tourists.

Terrifying Trivia

- Disney's *Pirates of the Caribbean* movies feature many ghost ship myths.

- The *Flying Dutchman* is believed to be cursed. The crew and captain of the ship are to sail the oceans forever.

- A girl named Jackie drowned in one of the *Queen Mary*'s pools. Some people claim to have seen her ghost wandering the pool area.

Glossary

aboard: on or in a boat

cargo: things stored on a boat

crew: people who work aboard a ship

drift: float with the current of the water

ghost: a spirit of a dead person

haunted: a space believed to be visited by spirits

mirage: something you see that isn't there

myth: a story about the past that may not be true

ship: a large boat

Further Reading

Kiddle: Ghost Facts for Kids
https://kids.kiddle.co/Ghost

Live Science: Erie! 6 Haunting Tales of Ghost Ships
https://www.livescience.com/48489-tales-of-ghost-ships.html

Marsico, Katie. *Undead Monsters: From Mummies to Zombies*. Minneapolis: Lerner Publications, 2017.

Pearson, Maggie. *Ghosts and Goblins: Scary Stories from around the World*. Minneapolis: Darby Creek, 2016.

Scary for Kids: Ghost Ships
http://www.scaryforkids.com/ghost-ships/

Index

Photo Acknowledgments

Image credits: Laura J Smith/Shutterstock.com, p. 4; zieusin/Shutterstock.com, pp. 5, 16; muratart/Shutterstock.com, p. 6; elena_akkurt/Stockphoto/Getty Images, p. 7; IgorZh/Shutterstock.com, p. 8; Hulton Archive/Getty Images, p. 9; DeAgostini/Getty Images, p. 10; Vadarshop/Shutterstock.com, p. 11; rangizzz/Shutterstock.com, p. 12; Michael Hall/Getty Images, p. 13; stockbob/Shutterstock.com, p. 14; sirtravelalot/Shutterstock.com, p. 15; Pobytov/DigitalVision Vectors/Getty Images, p. 17; ve Livesey/Getty Images, p. 18; Elenarts/Shutterstock.com, p. 19; Alfredo Schaufelberger/Shutterstock.com, p. 22.

Cover: RobertBreitpaul/iStockphoto/Getty Images; oleshko andrey/Shutterstock.com.

Main body text set in Billy Infant regular. Typeface provided by SparkType.